Text © 2022 by JoAnn Deak and Terrence Deak
Illustrations by Neely Daggett
Cover and internal illustrations and design © 2022 by Sourcebooks
Sourcebooks and the colophon are registered trademarks of Sourcebooks.
All rights reserved.
Photoshop and procreate were used to create the full color art.
Published by Sourcebooks eXplore, an imprint of Sourcebooks Kids
P.O. Box 4410, Naperville, Illinois 60567–4410
(630) 961-3900
sourcebookskids.com
Cataloging-in-Publication Data is on file with the Library of Congress.
Source of Production: 1010 Printing Asia Limited, Kwun Tong, Hong Kong, China
Date of Production: November 2021
Run Number: 5023856
Printed and bound in China.
OGP 10 9 8 7 6 5 4 3 2 1

GOOD NIGHT
TO YOUR
FANTASTIC
ELASTIC
BRAIN

A growth mindset book for kids about the amazing things your fantastic elastic brain does after you say good night.

WORDS BY
JoAnn Deak, PhD
Terrence Deak, PhD

PICTURES BY
Neely Daggett

sourcebooks
eXplore

The space behind your eyes and between your ears is filled with something that looks like a big pink walnut...**YOUR BRAIN.**

WHAT DOES THE BRAIN DO?

Your brain is like a living computer in your head with millions of little wirelike cells called neurons. These neurons work together to think, feel, move your body, and remember. Your brain does all the things that make you YOU.

NEURON

In other words, **YOU ARE YOUR BRAIN!**

KICK

KICK

KICK

After a long day, your body needs to rest and recover. Your body's daytime work is to do whatever you tell it to do: walk, run, play with your friends, and **LEARN**. Your body's nighttime work is to rest, recover, and **RECHARGE**.

It is called an organ, but in many ways the brain really acts like a muscle because as you grow, it strengthens. And the more you use it, the stronger it becomes!

Your brain has many different parts.
Each part has a SPECIAL JOB.

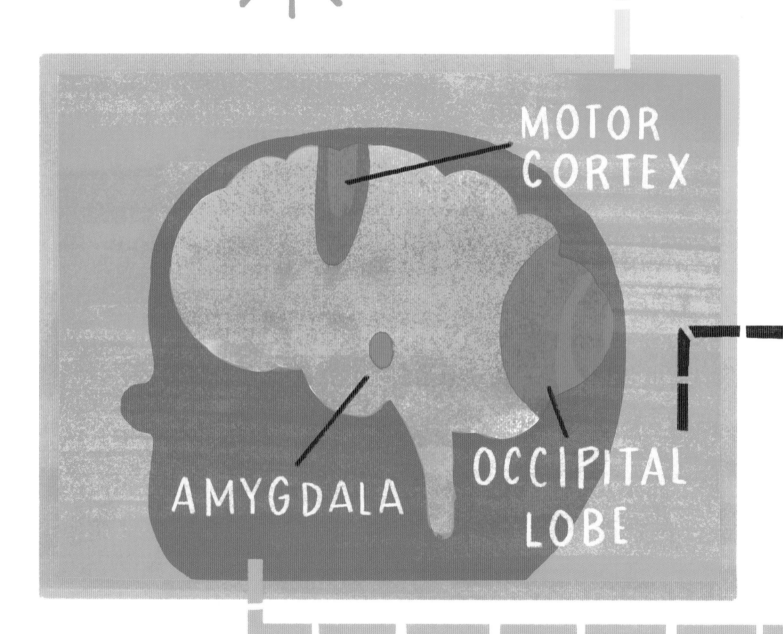

MOTOR
CORTEX

AMYGDALA

OCCIPITAL
LOBE

MOTOR CORTEX

There is a part across the middle of your head, from ear to ear, called the cortex, which controls your body. If you want to wave, that part of the brain sends a message to your hand to move.

OCCIPITAL LOBE

In the back of your head, there is a part of your brain called the occipital lobe. That part receives pictures from your eyes and tells you what you are seeing.

AMYGDALA

Deep in the middle of your brain is the amygdala (*uh-MIG-duh-luh*). This is where many of your feelings are, like fear. If something scares you, your amygdala is sending you that message.

PRACTICE MAKES PERMANENT!

Your brain acts like a muscle; the more you practice something you are learning, the better your brain will become at doing that task. Learning causes the brain to grow stronger. Your brain works hard every day and wants to be pushed and challenged to learn as much as possible.

YOUR BRAIN HELPS YOU...

PLAY VIOLIN,

LEARN HOW TO RIDE A BIKE,

OPEN YOUR EYES,

OR READ A BOOK!

By the time night comes, your brain and your body are getting tired and it is time to rest and recover.

BUT YOUR BRAIN IS DIFFERENT.

Even though your brain spent all day thinking, feeling, moving your body, learning, and remembering, its job is not done! Your brain can't stop working completely at night because it needs to keep your body functioning while you sleep.

Lower parts of your brain—the MEDULLA, located in the brain stem—tell your heart and lungs to slow down and relax. Since you won't be so active at night, you won't need so much energy and oxygen so your heart and lungs can slow a bit.

MEDULLA OBLONGATA

SLOW

Sleep is ubiquitous (*u-BICK-kwa-tus*). That's a wonderful, big word that describes sleep. It means that all animals sleep in some way.

BUGS SLEEP

FISH SLEEP

CATS SLEEP

AND BABIES SLEEP!

Even though you are not aware of all that is happening around you, your brain still responds to sights, sounds, and other things. Loud noises like that annoying alarm clock will wake you up because your ears still hear. Your parents gently touch your head or shoulder to wake you up because your skin still senses touch and motion. The smell of pancakes might wake you up because your nose always knows!

All of these things tell us that your brain is **STILL WORKING** when you sleep—even though it may take louder sounds, stronger rousing, or spicier smells to catch your attention than when you're awake.

BRAIN'S
NIGHTTIME CHECKLIST

- ★ develop
- ★ gain control
- ★ remember
- ★ forget
- ★ energize
- ★ take a bath
- ★ dream

Because your brain is so
helping you think, feel,
move during the day, it
its best work at night!

YOUR BRAIN DEVELOPS.

When you are born, you have billions of neurons with lots of bushy branches called DENDRITES. The tips of these branches make contact with other **NEURONS** at points called SYNAPSES, and this is how electrical impulses are transmitted to other neurons.

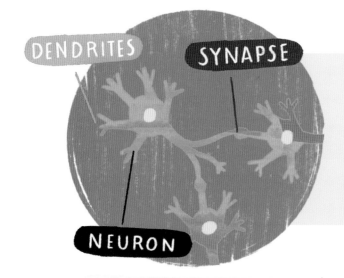

DENDRITES
SYNAPSE
NEURON

Over time, these connections between neurons become closer and stronger. This is partly because the number of synapses become "pruned."

Extra or unused synapses are sheared away like trimming the branches of a tree! While you sleep, glial cells help to prune unnecessary (or unused) synapses to strengthen important connections between neurons.

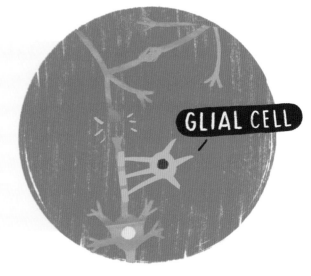

GLIAL CELL

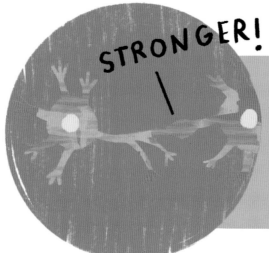

STRONGER!

This makes your brain work faster as you grow and develop.

So...unlike the trees in your yard that grow more branches with time, sleep helps your brain reduce its branches and strengthen the pathways used most often.

YOUR BRAIN GAINS CONTROL.

Being able to plan and make decisions is a big part of what makes us human. Planning your next move in a game or deciding what to wear happens in the prefrontal cortex, or PFC. This brain area develops rapidly as you grow and will continue to be sculpted until you are in your twenties! Right now the PFC is already playing a very important role in helping you make decisions, follow the rules, and think clearly about what you want to do in the future.

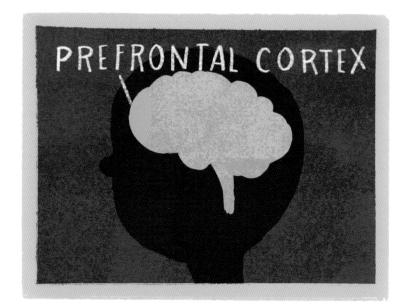

PREFRONTAL CORTEX

Getting a good night's sleep improves the processing power of your PFC and helps you take control of yourself!

YOUR BRAIN REMEMBERS.

Of all the things you learned while awake, your brain has to "stamp in" what you learned so that you don't forget. You don't know it's happening during sleep, but when you wake up and someone asks you where you went yesterday, you remember the details because they were "stamped in" while you slept.

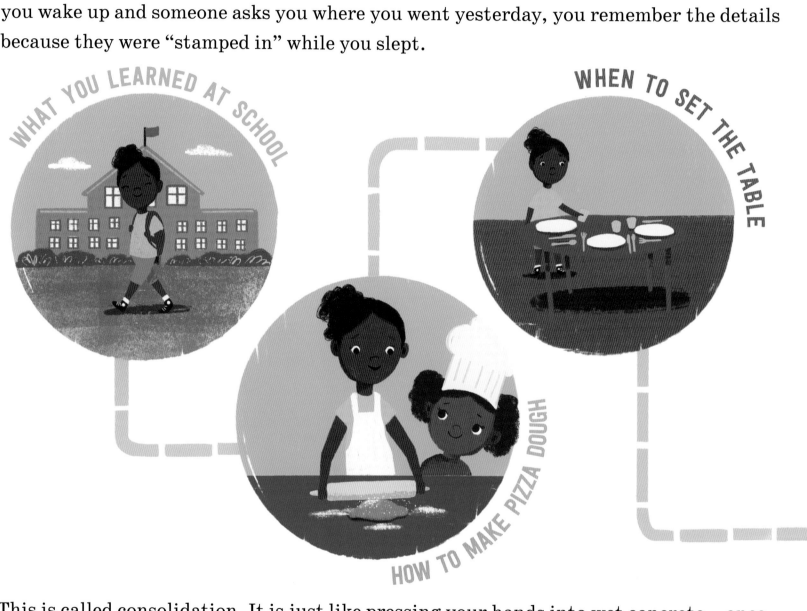

WHAT YOU LEARNED AT SCHOOL

WHEN TO SET THE TABLE

HOW TO MAKE PIZZA DOUGH

This is called consolidation. It is just like pressing your hands into wet concrete—once the concrete hardens, the hand prints are there to stay! Things you have learned need to "set" overnight so you can remember what you learned for years to come.
In many ways, we **SLEEP TO REMEMBER!**

A lot of information you learn requires your **HIPPOCAMPUS** because the neurons here are especially good at storing information about people, places, and events you experience.

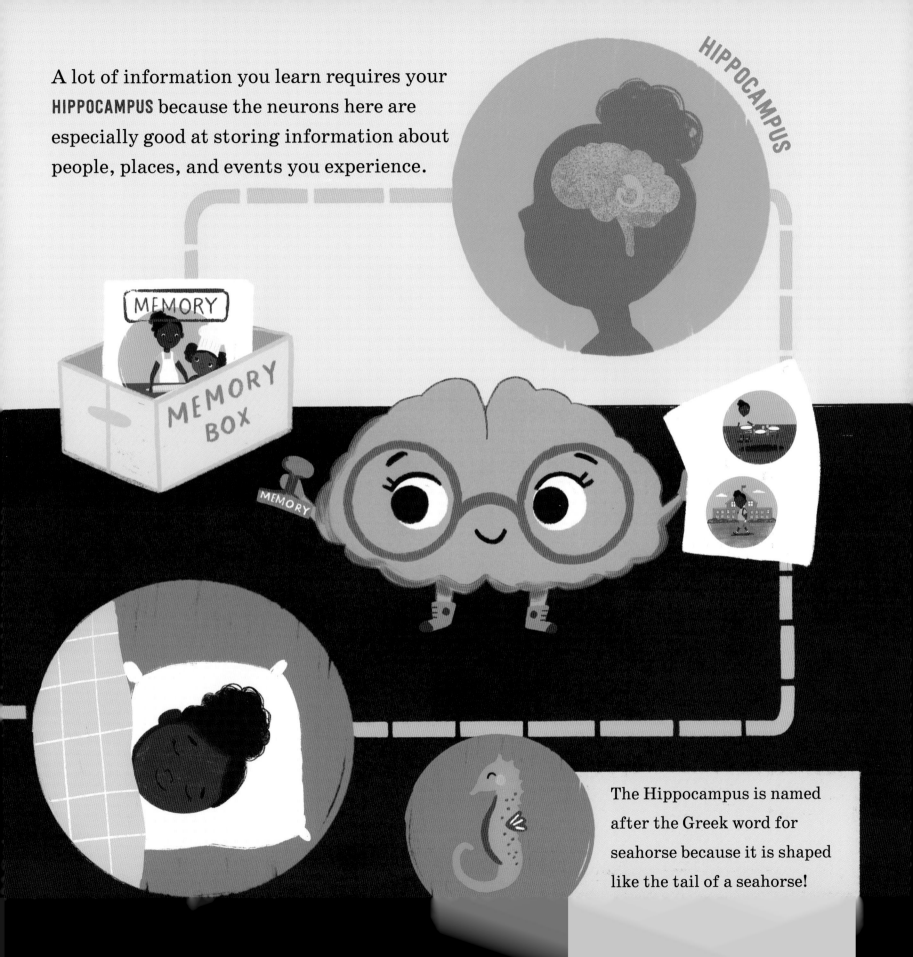

HIPPOCAMPUS

MEMORY

MEMORY BOX

MEMORY

The Hippocampus is named after the Greek word for seahorse because it is shaped like the tail of a seahorse!

YOUR BRAIN FORGETS.

Let's face it, sometimes we have a rough day. Sometimes we get scared by something that happens. Sometimes our feelings get hurt. These experiences are an important part of life and help us become **RESILIENT**, especially if we sleep well.

Did you know that sleep helps bad memories feel not so bad? We still remember those events, but the emotional part of the memory fades faster with a good night of sleep. But if we don't sleep well, these strong feelings stick around a whole lot longer. **WE SLEEP TO FORGET!**

YOUR BRAIN ENERGIZES.

Your brain is hungry all the time! It requires more blood flow to deliver oxygen and glucose (sugar)—two essential fuels for brain activity—than any other part of your body. To use those sugars as fuel, your body needs to "reset" every night while you sleep. If you sleep too little, you are likely to eat too much because your brain is not using sugar effectively. Sleep makes your brain (and body!) burn its fuel more efficiently so that you can RUN FARTHER, LEARN FASTER, AND BE MORE RESILIENT.

Your brain sleeps best when your dinner has been digested and your blood glucose has returned to normal levels. Sugary snacks and sweets right before bedtime can cause a surge in glucose that makes it harder to sleep consistently through the night.

YOUR BRAIN TAKES A BATH.

You have to take a bath or shower to get clean, which helps remove dirt and germs to help you stay healthy. Your brain is so busy during the day that it generates a lot of waste, which needs to be washed away at night.

The liquid in your head surrounding your brain is called cerebral spinal fluid (CSF). The day work of the CSF is to protect your soft brain from bumping into the hard bone of your head (your skull). The night work of the CSF is to flow through your brain like a bath or shower to clean it. Over your lifespan, your nightly brain baths that happen while you sleep will be important for healthy brain aging!

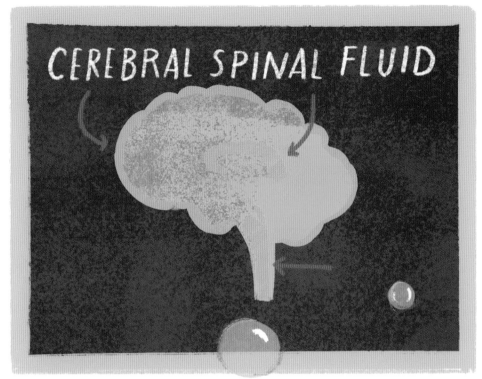

CEREBRAL SPINAL FLUID

YOUR BRAIN DREAMS.

We all dream, but scientists still know very little about why. Dreaming happens off and on throughout the night, with more dreams happening later in the night. During the most intense stage of sleep, your brain is the most active and your eyes wiggle back and forth quickly. This is why we call it the Rapid Eye Movement (REM) stage of sleep. Why do your eyes wiggle? No one knows! During REM sleep, your brain is very, very active, but the muscles in your arms, legs, fingers, and toes are unable to move. This is called REM paralysis and it is REALLY important for preventing you from acting out your dreams and getting injured. Imagine if you were dreaming about dancing on stage... without REM paralysis, you'd be doing pirouettes in your bed, not just in your head!

Even though the purpose of dreams is one of the greatest mysteries of our brain, we know REM sleep is essential. You can't live without it!

Have you ever watched a puppy sleep? You can see their eyes wiggling back and forth during REM sleep. Sometimes they will whimper and harrumph, their paws will twitch, and they might jerk their head a little. This happens because they are having a dream so intense that a little bit of muscle movement leaks out from under the REM paralysis!

We all sleep in different ways. We sleep best when we let our bodies follow a rhythm. This means we fall asleep and wake up at about the same time each day. Some people go to bed and sleep in late. Others go to bed and wake up early. But we all need sleep!

BABIES SLEEP THE MOST.

KIDS AND TEENS SLEEP A LOT.

THE AMOUNT OF SLEEP YOU NEED CHANGES AS YOU AGE.

ADULTS SLEEP LESS.

AS YOU BECOME ELDERLY, YOU NEED MORE SLEEP AND MIGHT EVEN START NAPPING AGAIN!

WHAT HAPPENS IF YOU DON'T GET ENOUGH SLEEP?

You forget...because your brain didn't have time to "stamp in" what you learned!

You make bad decisions... because your prefrontal cortex is too tired to think and plan!

You become impulsive... because your prefrontal cortex has a hard time controlling what you want to do!

You might get grouchy or emotional...because your amygdala, which controls emotions, becomes overactive!

You feel more pain...things that would normally cause a little pain (Ouch! I dropped a rock on my toe!) may make that pain feel unbearable!

You get very, very hungry...because your brain needs sleep to help use its fuel (sugar) efficiently!

Going to sleep at a regular time and getting the right amount of sleep is how you can help keep your brain growing and learning and elastic. A RESTED BRAIN IS A HEALTHY BRAIN, WHICH HELPS YOUR WHOLE BODY BE HEALTHIER.

For someone four to eight years old, it takes between ten and thirteen hours to do all of this night work.

TRAIN YOUR BRAIN: Going to bed at the same time every night is important. Why? You have this little part in the middle of your brain called the pineal gland. It makes a chemical that makes you sleepy, called melatonin (*mel-uh-TONE-in*). If you go to bed at the same time every night, the pineal gland learns what your bedtime is and will begin to produce melatonin to make it easier for you to fall asleep. You can train your brain when to sleep!

YOUR PINEAL GLAND LOOKS LIKE A PEA!

YOU ARE YOUR BRAIN. Everything you think and feel and do is controlled by your brain. You can build a better brain by taking care of your **SLEEP**, and now you know why!

Everyone needs regular sleep, because your brain has **MANY** important jobs that happen after you say good night. During sleep, your brain:

GROWS AND DEVELOPS

GAINS CONTROL

REMEMBERS AND FORGETS

ENERGIZES

TAKES A BATH

DREAMS

We know that you have the ability to help your brain grow by trying new things, making mistakes, and learning from your mistakes. But you have the power to train and grow your brain even more just by going to sleep! **GOOD NIGHT!**

NEURON